I0413106

Analysis of Dam-Passage Survival of Yearling and Subyearling Chinook Salmon and Juvenile Steelhead at The Dalles Dam, Oregon, 2010

By John W. Beeman, Tobias J. Kock , and Russell W. Perry, U.S. Geological Survey; and Steven G. Smith, National Oceanic and Atmospheric Administration-Fisheries

Prepared in cooperation with U.S. Army Corps of Engineers

Open-File Report 2011–1162

U.S. Department of the Interior
U.S. Geological Survey

U.S. Department of the Interior
KEN SALAZAR, Secretary

U.S. Geological Survey
Marcia K. McNutt, Director

U.S. Geological Survey, Reston, Virginia: 2011

For more information on the USGS—the Federal source for science about the Earth,
its natural and living resources, natural hazards, and the environment,
visit http://www.usgs.gov or call 1–888–ASK–USGS.

For an overview of USGS information products, including maps, imagery, and publications,
visit http://www.usgs.gov/pubprod

To order this and other USGS information products, visit http://store.usgs.gov

Suggested citation:
Beeman, J.W., Kock, T.J., Perry, R.W., and Smith, S.G., 2011, Analysis of dam-passage survival of yearling and
subyearling Chinook salmon and juvenile steelhead at The Dalles Dam, Oregon, 2010: U.S. Geological Survey
Open-File Report 2011-1162, 38 p.

Any use of trade, product, or firm names is for descriptive purposes only and does not imply
endorsement by the U.S. Government.

Although this report is in the public domain, permission must be secured from the individual
copyright owners to reproduce any copyrighted material contained within this report.

Contents

Figures

Tables

Conversion Factors

Inch/Pound to SI

Multiply	By	To obtain
foot (ft)	0.3048	meter (m)
mile (mi)	1.609	kilometer (km)
mile, nautical (nmi)	1.852	kilometer (km)
yard (yd)	0.9144	meter (m)

SI to Inch/Pound

Multiply	By	To obtain
meter (m)	3.281	foot (ft)

Analysis of Dam-Passage Survival of Yearling and Subyearling Chinook Salmon and Juvenile Steelhead at The Dalles Dam, Oregon, 2010

By John W. Beeman, Tobias J. Kock, and Russell W. Perry, U.S. Geological Survey; and Steven G. Smith, National Oceanic and Atmospheric Administration-Fisheries

Executive Summary

We performed a series of analyses of mark-recapture data from a study at The Dalles Dam during 2010 to determine if model assumptions for estimation of juvenile salmonid dam-passage survival were met and if results were similar to those using the University of Washington's newly developed ATLAS software. The study was conducted by the Pacific Northwest National Laboratory and used acoustic telemetry of yearling Chinook salmon, juvenile steelhead, and subyearling Chinook salmon released at three sites according to the new virtual/paired-release statistical model. This was the first field application of the new model, and the results were used to measure compliance with minimum survival standards set forth in a recent Biological Opinion. Our analyses indicated that most model assumptions were met. The fish groups mixed in time and space, and no euthanized tagged fish were detected. Estimates of reach-specific survival were similar in fish tagged by each of the six taggers during the spring, but not in the summer. Tagger effort was unevenly allocated temporally during tagging of subyearling Chinook salmon in the summer; the difference in survival estimates among taggers was more likely a result of a temporal trend in actual survival than of tagger effects. The reach-specific survival of fish released at the three sites was not equal in the reaches they had in common for juvenile steelhead or subyearling Chinook salmon, violating one model assumption. This violation did not affect the estimate of dam-passage survival, because data from the common reaches were not used in its calculation.

Contrary to expectation, precision of survival estimates was not improved by using the most parsimonious model of recapture probabilities instead of the fully parameterized model. Adjusting survival estimates for differences in fish travel times and tag lives increased the dam-passage survival estimate for yearling Chinook salmon by 0.0001 and for juvenile steelhead by 0.0004. The estimate was unchanged for subyearling Chinook salmon. The tag-life-adjusted dam-passage survival estimates from our analyses were 0.9641 (standard error [SE] 0.0096) for yearling Chinook salmon, 0.9534 (SE 0.0097) for juvenile steelhead, and 0.9404 (SE 0.0091) for subyearling Chinook salmon. These were within 0.0001 of estimates made by the University of Washington using the ATLAS software. Contrary to the intent of the virtual/paired-release model to adjust estimates of the paired-release model downward in order to account for differential handling mortality rates between release groups, random variation in survival estimates may result in an upward adjustment of survival relative to estimates from the paired-release model. Further investigation of this property of the virtual/paired-release model likely would prove beneficial. In addition, we suggest that differential selective pressures near release sites of the two control groups could bias estimates of dam-passage survival from the virtual/paired-release model.

Introduction

The 2008 Biological Opinion (BIOP) for the Federal Columbia River Power System set standards for juvenile salmonid dam-passage survival (National Marine Fisheries Service, 2008). The performance goals established in the BIOP specified that in order to demonstrate compliance with standards, statistical point estimates for dam-passage survival probability should be equal to or greater than 0.96 for yearling Chinook salmon (*Oncorhynchus tshawytscha*) and juvenile steelhead (*O. mykiss*), and equal to or greater than 0.93 for subyearling Chinook salmon. A Biological Assessment in 2007 specified standards for precision of estimates that had to be met in order to demonstrate compliance: standard error (SE) estimates should be equal to or less than 0.015 for all species (U.S. Army Corps of Engineers and others, 2007). The U.S. Army Corps of Engineers (USACE) must show empirically that survival standards are met at the dams they operate, with estimates that meet the precision standards.

Several variations of the classic Cormack-Jolly-Seber (Cormack, 1964; Jolly, 1965; and Seber, 1965) capture-mark-recapture statistical models have been used to estimate dam-passage survival in the Federal Columbia River Power System. Most models rely on paired releases of one group of fish released upstream of the dam (the 'treatment' group) and another released downstream of the dam (the 'control' group), from which a 'relative' survival estimate is calculated. The control group generally is released within a few hundred meters downstream of the dam. The estimated survival ratio of the two groups from their respective release points to a point downstream of the control release point provides an estimate of the survival over the spatial extent between the two release points; estimates of survival over this spatial extent are termed "dam survival" in the BIOP, which is the term we use in this report. Variations of this design have been described by Burnham and others (1987) and Skalski and others (2002). One potential shortcoming of this design is the potential for differential expression of post-release tagging and handling mortality between treatment and control groups, which could result in biased estimates of relative survival. For example, if treatment fish expressed this mortality prior to dam passage and control fish expressed it shortly after release, the relative survival estimate would be positively biased.

Skalski (2009) proposed a new design to address the effects of the potential differential expression of tagging and handling mortality between the control and treatment groups. The design relies on three release groups: one "released" upstream of the dam ("released" defined as those detected passing the dam; hence a "virtual" release group, V_1) and two released downstream. The downstream release groups are designed to remove the potential effects of tagging and handling—one group is released nearby the dam as in other models (R_1) and the other group (R_2) is released far enough downstream to expect that this mortality source has been expressed in the R_1. Dam survival is then expressed as survival of the V_1 group divided by survival ratios of the R_2 and R_3 groups, theoretically cancelling out the effects of short-term tagging and handling mortality (see table 1 in section, "Methods"). The first use of this design was in a study in 2010 at The Dalles Dam at Columbia River kilometer (rkm) 309. This first implementation also was the first study designed to evaluate compliance with the newly developed BIOP survival standards; additional model evaluations were added to the 2010 study at The Dalles Dam.

Evaluation of the model proposed by Skalski (2009) was conducted by several groups. The Pacific Northwest National Laboratory (PNNL) conducted fieldwork for the study, the University of Washington (UW) conducted the primary analysis to generate survival estimates, and the U.S. Geological Survey (USGS) and National Marine Fisheries Service (NMFS) conducted a parallel analysis to provide an independent assessment of the new survival model design (this report). The University of Washington developed software called ATLAS (Active Tag-Life Adjusted Survival), which they used to complete their analyses (Skalski, 2010; University of Washington, 2010). We analyzed the data independent from the ATLAS software. Details of the fieldwork portion of the research can be found in the proposal submitted to the USACE by PNNL in September 2009 (Carlson, 2009). Statistical results from the University of Washington will be available concurrently with this report, which summarizes statistical results from the USGS/NMFS analysis.

Methods

Study Design

In this section, we provide a general overview of the details of the acoustic telemetry evaluation that was conducted by PNNL during 2010 to evaluate dam-passage survival. This evaluation consisted of spring and summer study periods that occurred during April–June and June–August, respectively. Yearling Chinook salmon and juvenile steelhead were monitored during the spring study period and subyearling Chinook salmon were monitored during the summer study period. The goal of this section is to provide the reader with a general understanding of the study design. Specific details of the fieldwork conducted during 2010 can be obtained from Carlson (2009) and Carlson and Skalski (2010). The latter source describes results from the spring study period. A report from PNNL describing the summer study period results will be available at *http://www.nwp.usace.army.mil/environment/home.asp* when completed.

The study fish were collected at John Day Dam (rkm 348), surgically implanted with both acoustic transmitters and PIT tags, and released at one of three locations. Tagged yearling Chinook salmon and juvenile steelhead were released daily from April 28, 2010, to June 1, 2010, and tagged subyearling Chinook salmon were released daily from June 13, 2010 to July 17, 2010. The tagged fish were released into the Columbia River near Roosevelt, Washington (rkm 393), in the tailrace of The Dalles Dam near The Dalles, Oregon (rkm 307) and near Hood River, Oregon (rkm 275; fig. 1). The release site near Roosevelt, Washington, was chosen to meet the needs of this study and a concurrent study of dam passage at John Day Dam. The other release sites were selected to meet criteria associated with the virtual/paired-release model used for the study at The Dalles Dam (Skalski, 2009). Fish released near Roosevelt, Washington, were included in the analysis only if they were detected in the forebay of The Dalles Dam (rkm 309) and are hereafter referred to as the V_1 release group. Fish released near The Dalles, Oregon, were released at the downstream extent of the tailwater of The Dalles Dam at rkm 307 and are hereafter referred to as the R_2 release group. Fish released near Hood River, Oregon, were released at rkm 275 and are hereafter referred to as the R_3 release group.

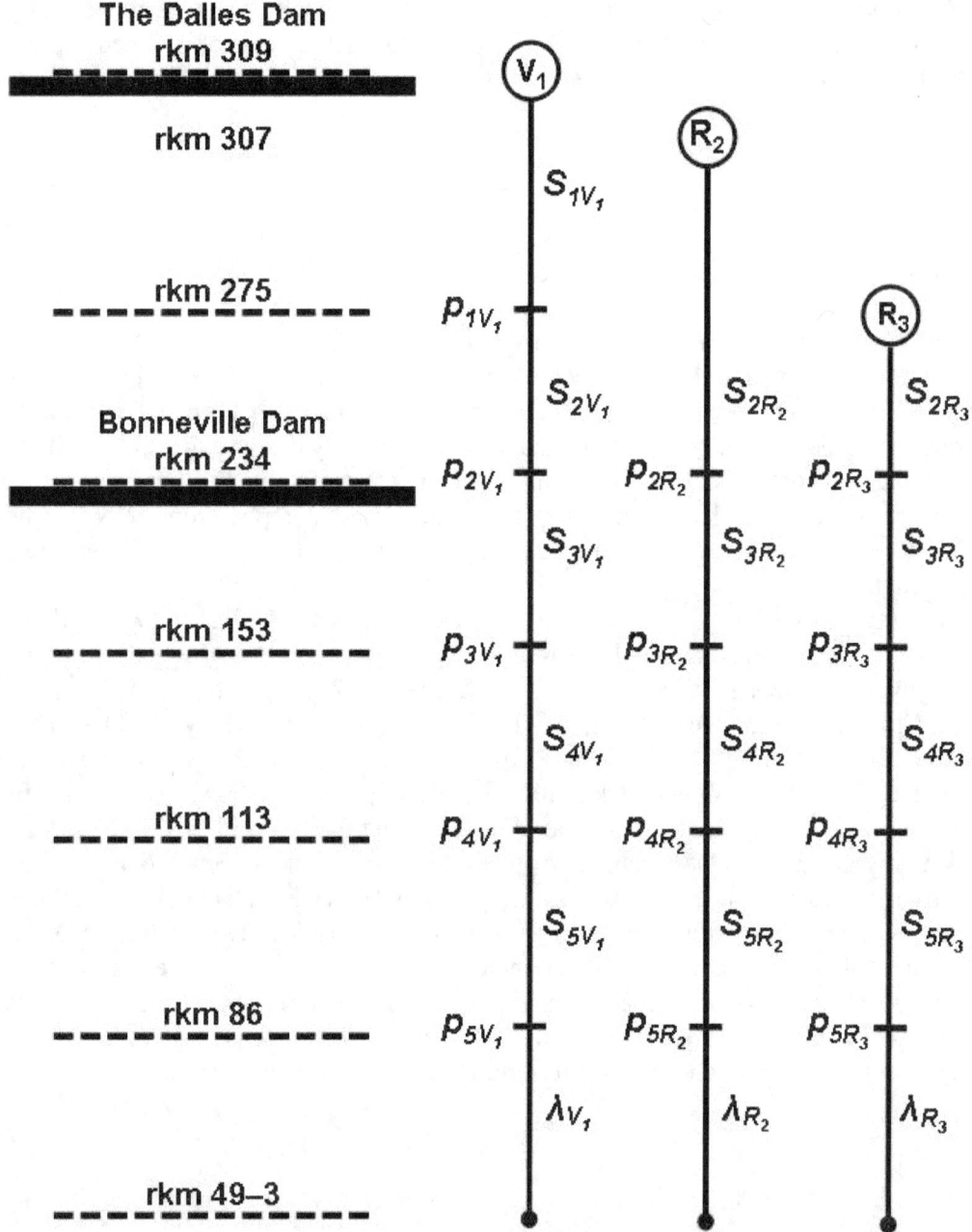

Figure 1. Schematic of the study design used to evaluate dam passage survival of juvenile salmonids at The Dalles Dam, Oregon, 2010. Unique detection (p) and survival (S) parameters are listed for each release group. Horizontal dashed lines represent acoustic tag detection sites used during the study. Release groups: V_1, fish released near Roosevelt, Washington; R_2, fish released near The Dalles, Oregon; R_3, fish released near Hood River, Oregon. Definition of survival and detection parameters are shown in table 1.

Acoustic telemetry receivers were deployed by PNNL at locations throughout the study area, which extended downstream of the release site near Roosevelt, Washington, to the mouth of the Columbia River. Primary monitoring arrays (hereafter referred to as sites) consisting of several acoustic telemetry receivers placed to detect tagged fish across part or all of the river width were located at rkm 309, 275, 234, 153, 113, 86, 49, 37, 22, 8, and 3 (fig. 1). For purposes of our analysis of detection histories, the six sites from rkm 309 to rkm 86 were selected as unique sites and data from the five sites from rkm 49 to rkm 3 were combined into a single detection "zone." Combining the lower river sites allowed use of the detection data in this portion of the river even though some of these sites did not span the entire river width. Thus, the detection histories consisted of seven characters that corresponded to release (the first digit) plus detection events at sites located at rkm 275, 234, 153, 113, 86, and 49–3.

Data Analysis

We examined acoustic telemetry and PIT-tag detection records to develop detection histories for each fish in the study. Proofed telemetry records provided by PNNL contained detection summaries of individual tagged fish. These summaries included the first and last detection time for each fish on a telemetry receiver in the study area, and the total number of valid detections of that fish on the receiver. For our analysis, acoustic detection data from telemetry receivers within each site were combined and fish that were detected at the site were coded with a "1" in the detection history. Fish that were not detected at a specific site were coded with a "0" for that site.

Some fish were censored prior to analysis. Information from PIT-tag detections was used to determine whether acoustic-tagged fish were diverted into sample tanks or sort-by-code tanks at John Day or Bonneville Dams. We assumed that fish diverted in such a way were not representative of the general population and were not reliable sources of information about survival downstream of the point of diversion. Thus, acoustic detection records for some fish were "censored" as follows: (1) records for fish diverted at John Day Dam were completely removed from the dataset; (2) records for fish diverted at Bonneville Dam were removed downstream of rkm 234. The sites selected for analyses and criteria used to develop capture histories were determined in cooperation with Dr. John Skalski at the University of Washington so that each group based their analyses on the same data. We used the User Specified Estimation Routine (USER) software program to estimate survival and detection parameters from the detection histories (Lady and others, 2003; table 1).

Table 1. Definitions of survival and detection parameters estimated by the virtual/paired-release model used in analyses of data from an acoustic-telemetry evaluation of dam-passage survival at The Dalles Dam, Oregon, 2010.

[Parameters listed are for the most general model possible (the "full" model). Special cases ("reduced" models) are possible by setting selected parameters equal to each other]

Parameter	Definition
S_1	Survival probability from the detection site in the forebay of The Dalles Dam to the detection site at rkm 275 for the V_1 release group only.
S_{2V1}	Survival probability from the detection site at rkm 275 to the detection site at rkm 234 for the V_1 release group.
S_{2R2}	Survival probability from the release location at rkm 307 to the detection site at rkm 234 for the R_2 release group.
S_{2R3}	Survival probability from the release location at rkm 275 to the detection site at rkm 234 for the R_3 release group.
S_{3r}	Survival probability from the detection site at rkm 234 to the detection site at rkm 153; r= V_1, R_2, or R_3.
S_{4r}	Survival probability from the detection site at rkm 153 to the detection site at rkm 113; r= V_1, R_2, or R_3.
S_{5r}	Survival probability from the detection site at rkm 113 to the detection site at rkm 86; r= V_1, R_2, or R_3.
λr	Conditional probability of being detected at least one site downstream of rkm 86, given survival to rkm 86. This probability involves both survival and detection probabilities r= V_1, R_2, or R_3
P_{1r}	Detection probability for the detection site at rkm 275 for the V_1 release group only.
P_{2r}	Detection probability for the detection site at rkm 234; r= V_1, R_2, or R_3.
P_{3r}	Detection probability for the detection site at rkm 153; r= V_1, R_2, or R_3.
P_{4r}	Detection probability for the detection site at rkm 113; r= V_1, R_2, or R_3.
P_{5r}	Detection probability for the detection site at rkm 86; r= V_1, R_2, or R_3.
S_{Dam}	Dam-passage survival through The Dalles Dam. Estimate is calculated using the following formula: $$\hat{S}_{Dam} = \frac{\hat{S}_1}{\left(\dfrac{\hat{S}_{2R2}}{\hat{S}_{2R3}}\right)}$$

Model Selection

Many of our analyses used an information-theoretic approach to compare and select among a set of hypotheses. The approach uses the principle of parsimony to compare mathematical models representing competing hypotheses regarding a dataset (for example, a fully parameterized, or "full" model, in which fish survival varies depending on who tagged the fish, versus a less parameterized, or "reduced" model, in which fish survival is identical among different taggers). Parsimony is the balance among bias, variance, and the number of parameters in a model: the square of bias is reduced as parameters are added to a model, but this increases the variance (Burnham and Anderson, 2002). There are several available measures of parsimony that can be used for this assessment. We chose the commonly used Akaike Information Criterion (AIC). Using this criterion, each model's parameters are fitted using the observed data using maximum-likelihood methods and the AIC value is computed. From the suite of models considered, the one with minimum AIC value is deemed "best"; that is, that model is best supported by the data. When comparing two specific models using AIC, unlike in the null hypothesis testing statistical framework, there is no strict cutoff representing a "significant" difference between models, however, guidelines for assessing support of a model or hypothesis by the data have been proposed. Burnham and Anderson (2002) suggest that when AIC values differ by less than 2 then support for the two hypotheses is not meaningfully different based on the data and models considered. In contrast, AIC differences of 10 or more indicate that one hypothesis is substantially better supported by the data than the other. We also used Likelihood Ratio tests of competing nested models to provide results based on a frequentist basis.

Model Assumptions

We examined several aspects of the data to determine if critical model assumptions were met during the study. Skalski (2009) listed 10 assumptions associated with the virtual/paired-release model used to estimate dam passage survival at The Dalles Dam during 2010. These are:

A1. Individuals marked for the study are a representative sample from the population of inference.
A2. All sampling events are "instantaneous." That is, sampling occurs over a negligible distance relative to the length of the intervals between sampling events.
A3. The fate of each tagged individual is independent of the fate of all others.
A4. All tagged individuals alive at a sampling location have the same probability of surviving until the end of that event.
A5. All tagged individuals alive at a sampling location have the same probability of being detected on that event.
A6. All tags are correctly identified and the status of smolt (that is, alive or dead), correctly assessed.
A7. Survival in the lower river segment of the first reach is conditionally independent of survival in the upper river segment.
A8. Releases V_1, R_1, and R_2 experience the same survival probabilities in the lower river segments they share in common.
A9. The virtual release group is constructed of tagged fish known to have passed through the dam.
A10. All fish arriving at the dam have an equal probability of inclusion in the virtual release group, independent of passage route through the dam.

In addition to these assumptions, the use of more than one person tagging fish introduces another potential source of bias. We therefore also examined the data for effects based on the tagger. The same also is true of tags from different manufacturing lots, but all tags in this study were from the same lot within study periods.

We identified several testable assumptions from the list above and performed a series of analyses to determine if they were met. The following questions were addressed in these analyses:
1. Were tagger effects apparent?
2. Were release groups adequately mixed throughout the study area (assumption A8)?
3. Were reach survival estimates equal among release groups (assumption A8)?
4. Did tag life meet or exceed fish travel times through the study area (assumption A6)?
5. Were euthanized tagged fish detected (assumption A6)?

Burnham and others (1987) proposed two tests to evaluate specific model assumptions ("Test2" and "Test3"), but we did not presented results of those tests in this report. The tests were designed to examine whether upstream or downstream detections affect downstream survival and/or detection (Test 2) and whether upstream capture histories affect downstream survival and/or capture (Test 3). These tests generally are performed in mark-recapture evaluations where physical handling of marked individuals is required to identify recapture events. In telemetry evaluations, the "recapture" events occur through a non-handling process in which a telemetry receiver detects a signal from an active transmitter (one with an internal power supply emitting a signal) and records the event. Additionally, the high detection probabilities typically associated with telemetry monitoring systems often results in data that are inadequate for conducting many of the tests, because few fish pass sites undetected. For example, we attempted to conduct a total of 60 Chi-squared tests using data from yearling Chinook salmon and juvenile steelhead, of which 27 could not be calculated because of inadequate data (typically zeros in rows or columns of contingency tables).

Tagger Effects

Tagging was accomplished by PNNL using six taggers during the spring study and seven during the summer study. We conducted a series of analyses to determine if tagger-specific factors were apparent in the data. One tagger only tagged fish during the spring and two taggers only tagged fish during the summer. We numbered taggers uniquely for identification, resulting in a total of eight tagger numbers. We examined the allocation of tagging effort by each tagger on a temporal scale as well as by release group. Comparisons along a temporal scale were made by visual examination of a table of the numbers of fish tagged by each tagger on each date. For the comparisons by release group, we used a Chi-squared contingency-table test ($\alpha=0.05$) to determine if the proportion of fish that were tagged by individuals similar among V_1, R_2, and R_3 release groups. We also compared reach-specific survival estimates by tagger to determine if the data supported differences in survival based on the tagger. This analysis was based on information-theoretic methods (Burnham and Anderson, 2002), but as mentioned previously, Likelihood Ratio tests also were conducted. We compared models representing the hypotheses that reach survivals of tagged fish differed among taggers (for example, $S_{2V1tagger1} \neq S_{2V1tagger2} \neq S_{2V1tagger3} \neq S_{2V1tagger4} \neq S_{2V1tagger5} \neq S_{2V1tagger6}$; the "full" model) or were equal among taggers (for example, $S_{2V1tagger1} = S_{2V1tagger2} = S_{2V1tagger3} = S_{2V1tagger4} = S_{2V1tagger5} = S_{2V1tagger6}$; a "reduced" model). Survival probabilities were fixed to 1 for analysis and the number of estimable parameters was reduced accordingly in cases where detection histories indicated no mortality occurred in the sample.

Mixing of Release Groups

At each site, we examined patterns in the detections of each release group through time to determine if release groups were adequately mixed during the study period. Cumulative passage distributions were generated and plotted by detection date for each release group at sites located at rkm 275, 234, 153, 113, and 86. A visual analysis of the detection patterns was then conducted to determine if release groups were passing sites similarly throughout the study period.

Model assumptions about survival parameters among groups also were evaluated using the information-theoretic approach. Once model assumptions were evaluated, we used the fully parameterized model to provide survival parameter estimates of interest, as this was consistent with the University of Washington method (B. Eppard, U.S. Army Corps of Engineers, written commun., September 1, 2010). We considered the following suite of models:

Model S1: Full model for survival probabilities. Unique parameter S_{ir} for each $i = 2, 3, 4, 5$ and $r = V_1$, R_2, or R_3.

Model S2: Survival probabilities vary by reach, but equal for different release groups in each reach beginning at rkm 234; $S_{iV1} = S_{iR2} = S_{iR3} = S_i$ for $i = 3, 4, 5$.

If model S2 was not supported, then we also considered models of different survival probabilities by reach, but equal among release groups in one of the last three reaches; $S_{iV1} = S_{iR2} = S_{iR3}$ for $i = 3$, or 4, or 5. These models were used to determine if the survival probabilities were equal among release groups in any one of the last three reaches.

Euthanized tagged fish were released by PNNL to allow assumption A6 to be evaluated, but no euthanized tagged fish were detected during the study and no evaluation was required.

Using Parsimony to Select Models of Detection and Survival Probabilities

We evaluated a suite of models of detection probabilities to determine which was the most supported by the data. This was done to determine if more parsimonious models were better supported by the data than the full model, and if so, if results from those models would provide an improvement in the precision of the survival estimates. While holding the model of survival probabilities constant (we used the full model of survival probabilities), we used AIC to identify the best-supported model for detection probabilities from among the following candidates:

Model P1: Full model for detection probabilities. Unique parameter for P_{ir} for each $i = 2, 3, 4, 5$ and $r = V_1, R_2$, or R_3.

Model P2: Detection probabilities vary by site, but equal for different release groups at each site; $P_{iV1} = P_{iR2} = P_{iR3} = P_i$ for $i = 2, 3, 4, 5$.

Model P3: Detection probabilities vary by release group, but equal across sites for each group; $P_{2r} = P_{3r} = P_{4r} = P_{5r} = P_r$ for $r = V_1, R_2$, or R_3.

Model P4: Detection probabilities equal for all groups and across sites; $P_{ir} = P$, for all $i = 2, 3, 4, 5$ and $r = V_1, R_2$, or R_3.

Detection probabilities were fixed to 1 for analysis and the number of estimable parameters was reduced accordingly in cases where detection histories indicated all fish in the sample were detected.

We also used the principle of parsimony to assess the assumption of equal survivals among release groups in common reaches. We used the most parsimonious models of detection probabilities and the same survival models described in section, "Equal Survival of Release Groups in Common Reaches" to estimate reach-specific group survivals as an aid in evaluating the equal survival assumption. We estimated reach-specific group survivals after model-averaging estimates from the models in the suite examined. Burnham and Anderson (2002) suggest that model selection uncertainty is indicated when AIC values of models differ by less than about 10. In the presence of model selection uncertainty, model-averaging acknowledges that inferences from a single model may be inappropriate and incorporates predicted survivals from all models into a series of model-averaged estimates. We followed the methods of Burnham and Anderson (2002), including averaging parameter estimates based on the model weights and averaging the standard errors based on their equation 6.12. Model averaging also inflates standard errors to account for model selection uncertainty.

Tag Life Adjustments and Dam Survival Estimates

An adjustment to the dam-survival estimate was made to reduce the bias due to potential differences between fish travel times and tag lives. The adjustment was applied to the reach-survival estimates that were used to estimate dam survival and the associated variance was applied to the dam-survival estimate. We used bootstrap techniques to estimate the variance of adjusted dam survival based on the conditional variance formula provided by equations B.20–22 in Appendix B of the ATLAS software manual (Lady and others, 2010). We used a slightly different approach to estimate the variance components than the approach that was presented in Lady and others (2010). Dam survival adjusted for tag life was estimated by

1. Estimating apparent survival as the joint probability of fish survival and "tag" survival ($\hat{T}_i$) in an ordinary Cormack-Jolly-Seber model,

2. Adjusting for tag failure by dividing apparent survival probabilities in each reach by $\hat{T}_i$, and

3. Estimating dam survival from the adjusted reach-survival estimates.

The variance of dam survival was calculated using bootstrap techniques to incorporate variance in $\hat{T}_i$ due to uncertainty in travel times and the tag survival curve. Equation 21 in Skalski (2010) partitions the variance of survival into two sources. The first source is the variance in survival conditional on the observed tag-life probabilities. We estimated this source of variance by using the Delta method (Seber, 1982) to estimate the variance of adjusted dam survival, assuming the tag-life probabilities as known constants. The second source of error arises due to uncertainty in travel times and the fitted tag survival curve. This source of variance was estimated using equation 22 in Skalski (2010). This approach required bootstrapping the tag life data and travel times associated with the three reach survival estimates that comprise dam survival. For each bootstrapped tag life and travel time dataset (we used 1,000 bootstrap datasets), the vitality model of Li and Anderson (2009) was re-fit to the data, $\hat{T}_i$ was recalculated, and adjusted dam survival was estimated as described above.

Results

The analyses were based on 3,603 yearling Chinook salmon, 3,645 juvenile steelhead, and 4,117 subyearling Chinook salmon (appendixes A, B, and C). These numbers do not include seven fish censored after entering the sample tank or sort-by-code system at John Day Dam. The numbers of tagged fish released in each group were similar among species. Yearling Chinook salmon were comprised of 2,037 fish in the V_1 group, 769 in the R_2 group, and 797 in the R_3 group. Juvenile steelhead were comprised of 2,048 fish in the V_1 group, 799 in the R_2 group, and 798 in the R_3 group. Subyearling Chinook salmon were comprised of 2,517 fish in the V_1 group, and 800 fish in each of the R_2 and R_3 groups. Few of the potential detection histories were represented. The most common detection history of the V_1, R_2, and R_3 groups represented fish released and detected at all sites downstream.

Model Assumptions

Tagger Effects

The fish tagged by each tagger were divided similarly among the three release groups. During the spring, each person tagged 13.6–20.4 percent of each yearling Chinook salmon or juvenile steelhead release group (table 2). During the summer, tagger #8 tagged 4.4–6.0 percent and the rest tagged 12.9–18.2 percent of each subyearling Chinook salmon release group. The Chi-squared tests indicated no difference in the proportions of the three release groups of yearling Chinook salmon ($\chi^2 = 1.03$, df, $= 10$, $P = 0.9998$), juvenile steelhead ($\chi^2 = 0.59$, df $= 10$, $P = 1.000$), or subyearling Chinook salmon ($\chi^2 = 8.54$, df $= 12$, $P = 0.7420$) tagged by each person.

The disparity between overall tagging efforts among taggers in the summer prompted us to examine the effort along a temporal scale. During the spring, the temporal effort was similar among taggers with a schedule of about 8–9 days of tagging followed by 2–3 days not tagging (appendixes D and E). During the summer, the temporal tagging effort was not similar among taggers (appendix F). During the summer, tagger #1 did not tag fish from May 12–28 and tagger #8 did not tag fish after June 23. In addition, taggers #2, #6, and #8 had longer periods without tagging than during the spring schedule.

Table 2. Percentages of study fish that were tagged by different taggers and released at three locations during an acoustic telemetry evaluation of dam-passage survival at The Dalles Dam, Oregon, 2010.

[Numbers of fish tagged are shown in parentheses. Tagger #5 did not tag subyearling Chinook salmon and taggers #7 and #8 did not tag yearling Chinook salmon or juvenile steelhead]

Tagger #	Roosevelt	The Dalles	Hood River
	Yearling Chinook salmon		
1	19.3% (441)	18.7% (149)	19.1% (152)
2	15.5% (356)	15.5% (123)	15.8% (126)
3	13.6% (311)	13.8% (110)	13.7% (109)
4	15.3% (350)	16.2% (129)	14.7% (117)
5	16.3% (372)	15.6% (124)	16.3% (130)
6	20.0% (457)	20.2% (161)	20.4% (163)
Totals	100.0% (2,287)	100.0% (796)	100.0% (797)
	Juvenile steelhead		
1	18.8% (430)	19.4% (155)	19.6% (157)
2	15.6% (359)	15.5% (124)	15.2% (121)
3	14.5% (331)	14.3% (114)	14.0% (112)
4	15.5% (354)	15.8% (126)	15.8% (126)
5	16.0% (365)	15.6% (125)	15.8% (126)
6	19.6% (449)	19.4% (155)	19.6% (156)
Totals	100.0% (2,288)	100.0% (799)	100.0% (798)
	Subyearling Chinook salmon		
1	16.4% (467)	18.2% (146)	17.4% (139)
2	17.2% (489)	16.9% (135)	16.6% (133)
3	15.9% (454)	15.4% (123)	14.9% (119)
4	16.3% (463)	14.5% (116)	16.0% (128)
6	12.9% (369)	13.5% (108)	14.4% (115)
7	15.3% (436)	16.5% (132)	16.3% (131)
8	6.0% (171)	5.0% (40)	4.4% (35)
Totals	100.0% (2,849)	100.0% (800)	100.0% (800)

The data did not support an effect of tagger identity on estimates of yearling Chinook salmon or juvenile steelhead survival, but did support an effect on subyearling Chinook salmon survival. The models describing survival of yearling Chinook salmon varying among taggers were not supported relative to those describing equal survival of fish among taggers (table 3). The delta AIC value was 61.9, indicating virtually no support for different survivals based on tagger identity. The result was similar for data from juvenile steelhead, where the delta AIC was 57.7. These results were corroborated by those from Likelihood Ratio tests for yearling Chinook salmon ($P = 0.94$) and juvenile steelhead ($P = 0.81$) indicating that the full models were not supported relative to the reduced models. The delta AIC from the subyearling Chinook salmon comparison was 8.9, also indicating little support for differences in reach survival of fish among taggers. However, in this case the Likelihood Ratio test indicated support for different survivals among taggers ($P = 0.0001$). The survival of fish tagged by tagger #1 was generally lower, and survival of those tagged by tagger #8 generally was higher than those of the other taggers (table 4). The disparity in schedules of tagger #1 and #8 likely contributed to these patterns, because survival of subyearling Chinook salmon is often inversely related to water temperature or season and thus decreases over time. This result prompted communication with University of Washington and subsequently additional analyses on their part to determine if the effect was due to tagger or temporal effects. Their analyses indicated the two factors were confounded and their effects could not be separately estimated (J. Skalski, University of Washington, written commun., November 5, 2010). We therefore based subsequent analyses on all fish tagged.

Mixing of Release Groups

The data suggest that release groups were adequately mixed across the study periods and throughout the study area. Visual assessment of cumulative passage distribution plots showed that yearling Chinook salmon and juvenile steelhead were passing detection arrays primarily during May, and that cumulative passage among the release groups was similar at each array (figs. 2 and 3). The groups of subyearling Chinook salmon were passing the sites in June and July and cumulative passage of all three groups were similar at each site (fig. 4).

Table 3. Models used to evaluate hypotheses about potential tagger effects from an acoustic telemetry evaluation of dam-passage survival at The Dalles Dam, Oregon, 2010.

[Data include Akaike's information criterion (AIC), the differences in AIC relative to the AIC best model in the set (Delta AIC), the number of parameters estimated by each model (K), the log-likelihood (LL), and results from likelihood ratio tests (LRT). Df denotes degrees of freedom, P denotes probability, and na denotes not applicable]]

Model No.	Hypothesis	AIC	Delta AIC	K	LL	LRT χ^2(df)	P
				Yearling Chinook salmon			
1	Different survival among taggers	1,143.63	61.9	150	-421.81	na	na
2	Equal survival among taggers	1,081.70	0.0	102	-438.85	34.08 (48)	0.9354
				Juvenile steelhead			
3	Different survival among taggers	1,320.63	57.7	153	-507.32	na	na
4	Equal survival among taggers	1,262.97	0.0	104	-527.49	40.34 (49)	0.8062
				Subyearling Chinook salmon			
5	Different survival among taggers	1,461.65	8.9	182	-548.82	na	na
6	Equal survival among taggers	1,452.79	0.0	124	-602.4	107.16 (58)	0.0001

Table 4. Reach-specific survival estimates for subyearling Chinook salmon that were tagged by seven different taggers during an acoustic telemetry evaluation of dam-passage survival at The Dalles Dam, Oregon, 2010.

[Standard errors are shown in parentheses. Reach survival estimates were obtained from model 5 in table 3. Estimates without standard errors are those set to 1.000 for analysis due to the lack of mortality in the sample. Tagger #5 did not tag subyearling Chinook salmon and taggers #7 and #8 only tagged subyearling Chinook salmon]

Tagger #	Reach 1 rkm 309 to rkm 275	Reach 2 rkm 275 to rkm 234	Reach 3 rkm 234 to rkm 153	Reach 4 rkm 153 to rkm 113	Reach 5 rkm 113 to rkm 86
			V_1 releases		
1	0.8932 (0.0162)	0.9527 (0.0134)	0.8806 (0.0198)	0.9692 (0.0111)	0.9648 (0.0118)
2	0.9406 (0.0113)	1.0000	0.9592 (0.0101)	0.9909 (0.0053)	0.9980 (0.0027)
3	0.9041 (0.0154)	0.9524 (0.0123)	0.9126 (0.0168)	0.9732 (0.0106)	0.9746 (0.0101)
4	0.9468 (0.0113)	1.0000	0.9197 (0.0142)	0.9966 (0.0036)	0.9989 (0.0033)
6	0.9024 (0.0164)	0.9879 (0.0164)	0.9533 (0.0131)	0.9722 (0.0107)	0.9787 (0.0094)
7	0.9563 (0.0162)	1.0000	0.9783 (0.0133)	0.9822 (0.0125)	1.0000
8	0.9153 (0.0146)	0.9676 (0.0103)	0.9426 (0.0138)	0.9810 (0.0086)	0.9912 (0.0061)
			R_2 releases		
1		0.9584 (0.0180)	0.9226 (0.0237)	0.9777 (0.0138)	0.9592 (0.1811)
2		0.9581 (0.0178)	0.9619 (0.0183)	0.9814 (0.0136)	0.9842 (0.0121)
3		0.9787 (0.0141)	0.9637 (0.0178)	1.0000	0.9671 (0.0178)
4		0.9721 (0.0174)	0.9421 (0.0239)	0.9925 (0.0118)	0.9511 (0.0226)
6		0.9818 (0.0130)	0.9902 (0.0098)	1.0000	1.0000
7		1.0000	1.0000	1.0000	1.0000
8		0.9733 (0.0151)	0.9511 (0.0202)	0.9925 (0.0099)	0.9761 (0.0155)
			R_3 releases		
1		1.0000	0.9369 (0.0210)	0.9753 (0.0141)	0.9844 (0.0111)
2		0.9948 (0.0076)	0.9691 (0.0161)	0.9832 (0.0121)	0.9980 (0.0089)
3		0.9872 (0.0121)	0.9616 (0.0189)	1.0000	1.0000
4		0.9987 (0.0084)	0.9289 (0.0251)	0.9685 (0.0179)	1.0000
6		0.9834 (0.0122)	0.9837 (0.0132)	0.9889 (0.1112)	1.0000
7		1.0000	1.0000	1.0000	1.0000
8		0.9807 (0.0133)	0.9669 (0.0172)	0.9834 (0.0126)	0.9496 (0.020)

The data and models support equal reach survivals among release groups for yearling Chinook salmon, but not for juvenile steelhead or subyearling Chinook salmon. For yearling Chinook salmon, the model describing equal reach survivals among groups in each of the S_3, S_4, and S_5 reaches was supported. The delta AIC between this and the full model was 6.81 in favor of the reduced model, indicating considerable support for equal survivals among the groups in the reaches in which they travelled the same distance (table 5). The data and models did not support equal group survivals of juvenile steelhead within these reaches. The difference in AIC between the full model (model 7) and the reduced model (model 8) of juvenile steelhead was 4.53 in favor of the full model, indicating moderate support for the hypothesis that group survivals differed within reaches. However, several other competing models were supported nearly as well as the full model, indicting support for the hypothesis that survival was not equal in all reaches.

Results from subyearling Chinook salmon data indicated that the survivals were not unequivocally equal in the reaches they had in common. The model describing equal survival in common reaches (model 13) and one describing equality only in S_4 (model 16) were both well supported, with AIC values within 1.58 of one another. These models were better supported than the others by 3.37–7.27 AIC units, indicating moderate support for some of the other hypotheses as well. The Likelihood Ratio test results indicated the hypothesis of equal survivals in S_3, S_4, and S_5 is not supported relative to the full model ($P = 0.0037$), and that the hypothesis of equal survival in S_4 is more supported than the full model ($P = 0.2988$).

Using Parsimony to Select Models of Detection and Survival Probabilities

A suite of models of detection and survival probabilities were evaluated to determine if reliance on only the full models for evaluating assumptions and estimating survival probabilities was adequate. Reduced models of detection probabilities were considered to determine if precision of survival estimates could be improved and reduced models of and survival probabilities were considered to address model selection uncertainty in assessing the similarity of reach-specific survival estimates.

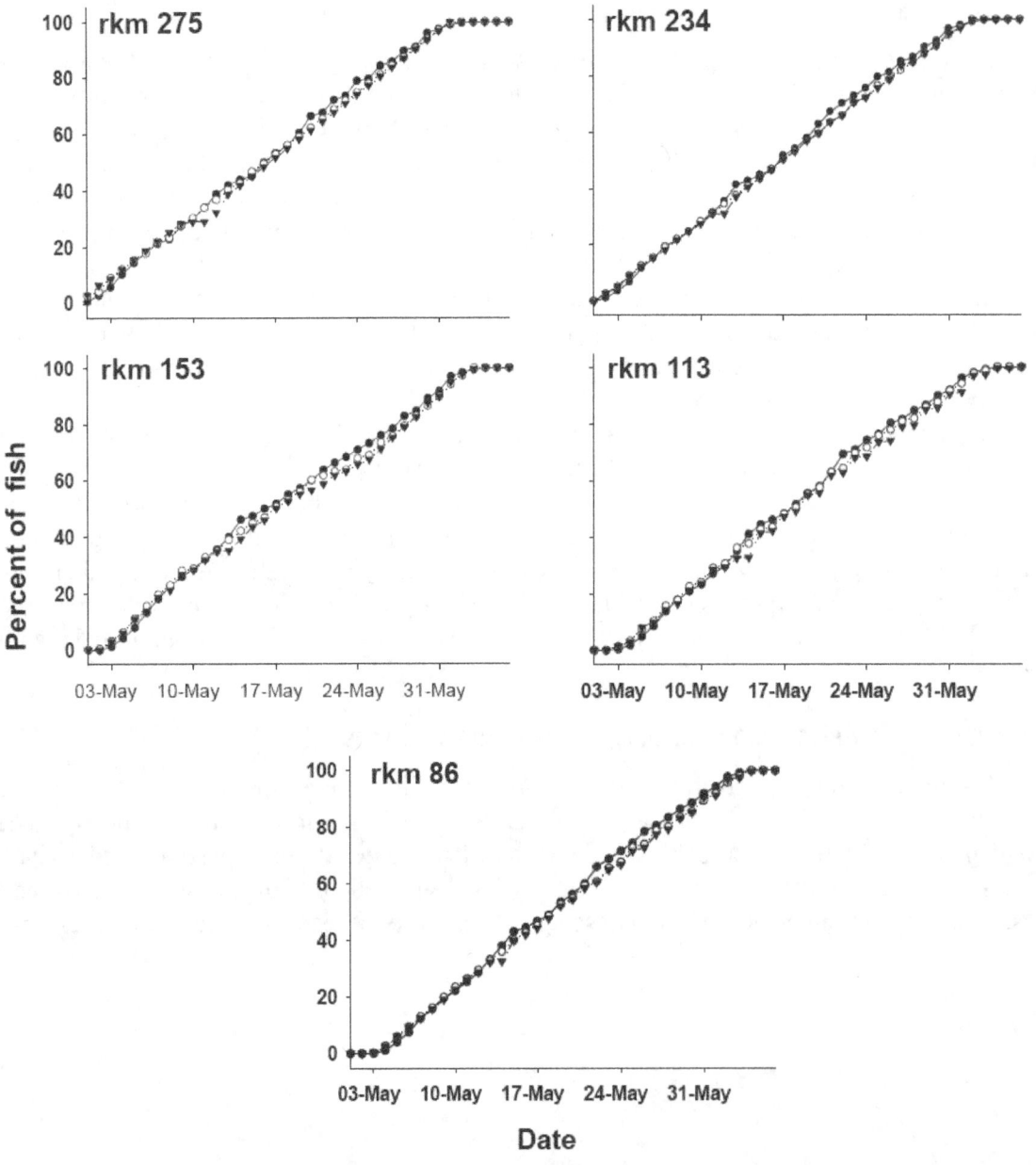

Figure 2. Cumulative passage distributions of acoustic-tagged yearling Chinook salmon at acoustic sites in the Columbia River, 2010. Data are from groups of fish that were released near Roosevelt, Washington (filled circles), The Dalles, Oregon (open circles), and Hood River, Oregon (filled triangles).

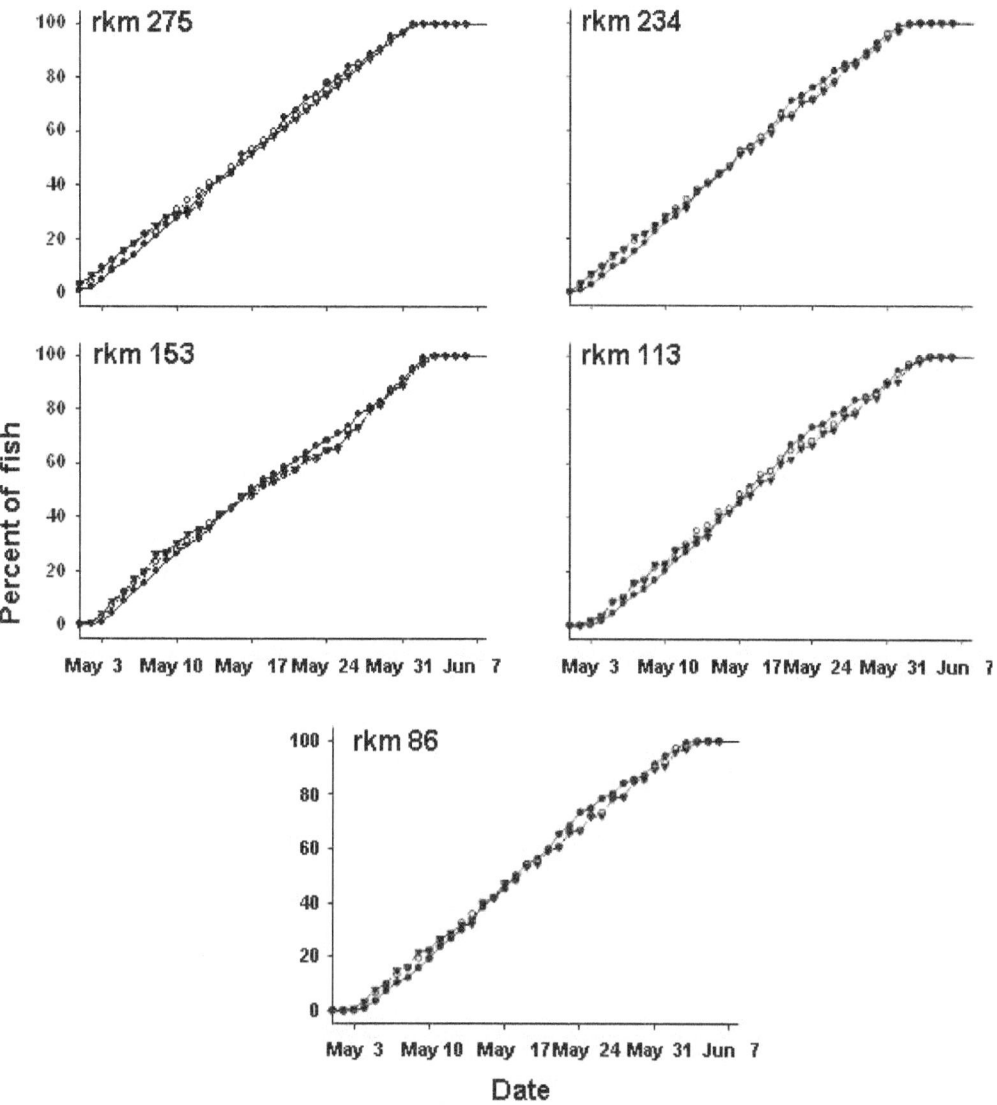

Figure 3. Cumulative passage distributions of acoustic-tagged juvenile steelhead at acoustic sites in the Columbia River, 2010. Data are from groups of fish that were released near Roosevelt, Washington (filled circles), The Dalles, Oregon (open circles), and Hood River, Oregon (filled triangles).

17

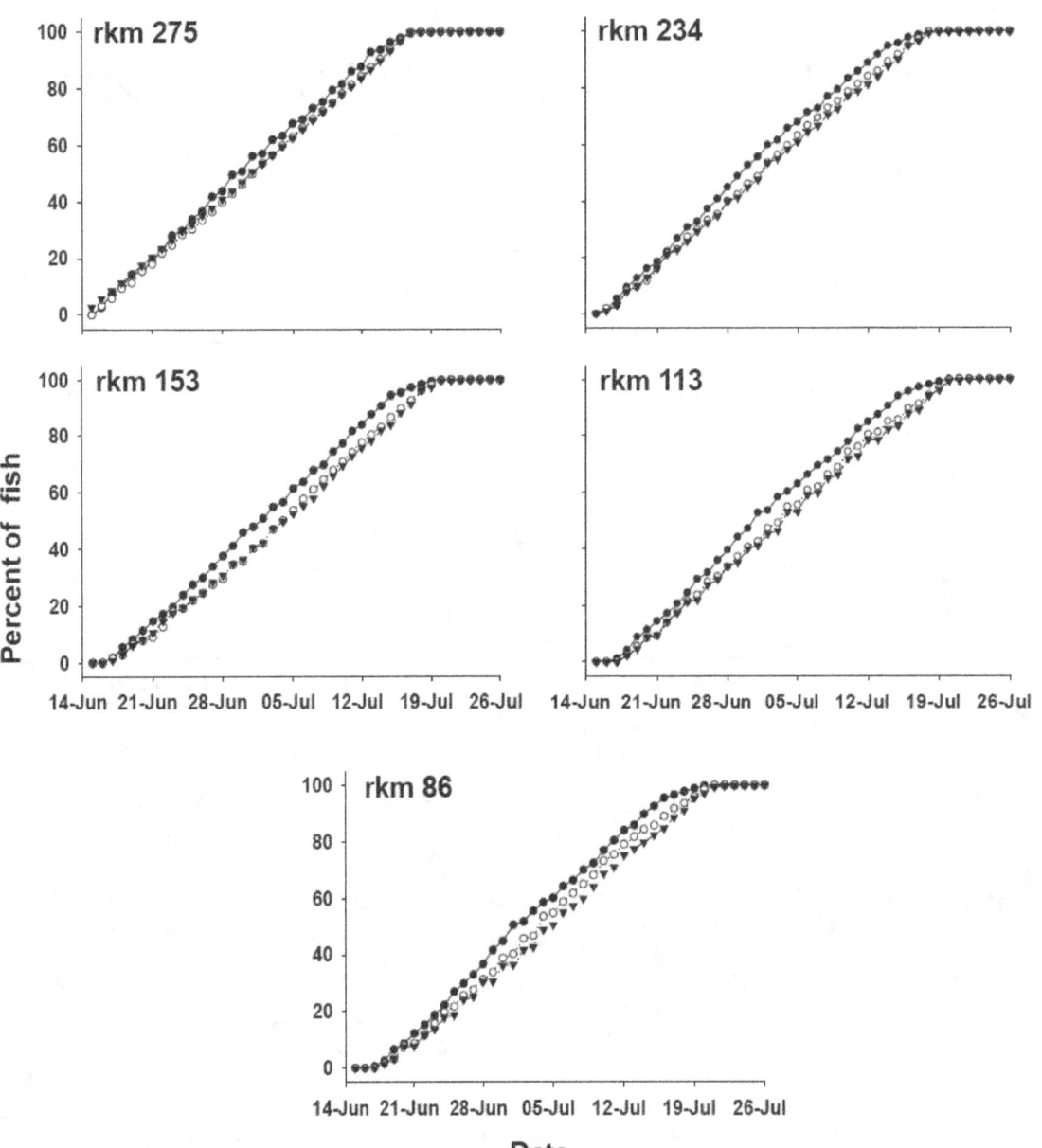

Figure 4. Cumulative passage distributions of acoustic-tagged subyearling Chinook salmon at acoustic sites in the Columbia River, 2010. Data are from groups of fish that were released near Roosevelt, Washington (filled circles), The Dalles, Oregon (open circles), and Hood River, Oregon (filled triangles).

Table 5. Models used to evaluate hypotheses about the equality of reach-specific survivals of release groups in reaches they had in common from an acoustic telemetry evaluation of dam-passage survival at The Dalles Dam, Oregon, 2010.

[Data include Akaike's information criterion (AIC), the differences in AIC relative to the AIC best model in the set (Delta AIC), the number of parameters estimated by each model (K), the log-likelihood (LL), and results from likelihood ratio tests (LRT). All models share a common model of detection probabilities allowing different probabilities among groups and reaches (the full model). Df denotes degrees of freedom, P denotes probability, and na denotes not applicable]

Model No.	Hypothesis	AIC	Delta AIC	K	LL	LRT χ^2(df)	P
			Yearling Chinook salmon				
5	Groups differ within all reaches	326.86	6.81	31	-132.43	na	na
6	Groups equal within S_3, S_4, S_5	320.05	0.00	25	-135.02	5.19 (6)	0.5202
			Juvenile steelhead				
7	Groups differ within all reaches	394.16	0.06	30	-167.08	na	na
8	Groups equal within S_3, S_4, S_5	398.69	4.59	24	-175.34	16.53 (6)	0.0112
9	Groups equal in S_5	396.52	2.43	28	-170.26	6.36 (2)	0.0415
10	Groups equal in S_4	394.10	0.00	28	-169.05	3.94 (2)	0.1397
11	Groups equal within S_3, S_4	395.54	1.44	26	-171.77	9.38 (2)	0.0523
12	Groups equal in S_3	394.73	0.63	28	-169.36	4.57 (4)	0.1018
			Subyearling Chinook salmon				
13	Groups differ within all reaches	397.50	1.58	31	-167.75	na	na
14	Groups equal within S_3, S_4, S_5	404.77	8.85	25	-177.38	19.27 (6)	0.0037
15	Groups equal in S_5	400.87	4.95	29	-171.43	7.37 (2)	0.0251
16	Groups equal in S_4	395.92	0.00	29	-168.96	2.42 (2)	0.2988
17	Groups equal within S_3, S_4	401.70	5.78	27	-173.85	12.20 (4)	0.0160
18	Groups equal in S_3	402.68	6.77	29	-172.34	9.18 (2)	0.0101

Models of Detection Probabilities

Reduced models were the most parsimonious models of detection probabilities of yearling Chinook salmon and juvenile steelhead, suggesting that precision of the estimated survivals could be improved from those based on the full models (table 6). The hypothesis that detection probabilities were equal among groups but varied among sites was the only one supported by the data and the models from yearling Chinook salmon and juvenile steelhead (models 21 and 25). The AICs of these models were at least 9.70 lower than those of models describing the hypothesis that detection probabilities varied among both groups and sites (the full model), and were at least 1146.70 lower than models describing the other hypotheses. The conclusions based on the Likelihood Ratio tests were identical.

Data from subyearling Chinook salmon supported the hypothesis of equal detection probabilities among groups nearly as much as that of differing detection probabilities among groups (table 6). The delta AIC between the full model describing different detection probabilities among groups and sites (model 27) and the reduced model describing detection probabilities equal among groups and differing among sites (model 29) was 0.93, indicating considerable support for each hypothesis. Thus, the data and models indicate either hypothesis is plausible. The conclusions using Likelihood Ratio tests were similar, with moderate support for a similarity between the hypotheses ($P = 0.0576$). The other hypotheses were not supported by either method.

The estimated standard errors of the detection probabilities from the reduced models were slightly smaller from the full models. For example, the estimates of detection probabilities of yearling Chinook salmon groups at rkm 234 ranged from 0.9944 (SE 0.0028) to 0.9973 (SE 0.0019) from the full model (table 7) and were 0.9950 (SE 0.0012) from the reduced model (table 8). In general, detection probabilities were high and differed slightly among release groups at each site. Detection probabilities were highest in the upstream reaches of the study area and exceeded 0.9130, with the exception of the site located at rkm 153, which ranged from 0.7457 (SE 0.0106) to 0.8728 (SE 0.0122).

The reach-specific and dam-survival estimates based on full and reduced models of detection probabilities were similar. The reach-specific survival probabilities were within 0.0013 of one another for both species and the standard errors of the estimates were within 0.0002 of one another (tables 9 and 10). Most estimates of survival were within 0.0002 of one another, except for those from subyearling Chinook salmon. The estimates of dam survival for yearling Chinook salmon differed by 0.0002, those for juvenile steelhead were equal, and those for subyearling Chinook salmon differed by 0.0006. The standard errors of dam survivals from the full and reduced models were equal within species. Using the reduced model for detection probabilities did not improve the precision of the survival estimates. The comparisons were based on survival estimates prior to adjustments for tag life probabilities, but these adjustment are constants and do not affect the comparisons.

Table 6. Models used to evaluate hypotheses about detection probabilities from an acoustic telemetry evaluation of dam-passage survival at The Dalles Dam, Oregon, 2010.

[Data include Akaike's information criterion (AIC), the differences in AIC relative to the AIC best model in the set (Delta AIC), the number of parameters estimated by each model (K), the log-likelihood (LL), and results from likelihood ratio tests (LRT). Df denotes degrees of freedom, P denotes probability, and na denotes not applicable]

Model No.	Hypothesis	AIC	Delta AIC	K	LL	LRT χ^2(df)	P
			Yearling Chinook salmon				
19	Differ by group and site	326.86	12.20	32	-132.43	na	na
20	Differ by group, equal by site	1461.37	1146.70	21	-709.68	1154.50 (11)	<0.0001
21	Equal by group, differ by site	314.64	0.00	23	-134.32	3.78 (9)	0.9253
22	Equal by group and site	1481.73	1167.10	19	-721.87	1178.88 (13)	<0.0001
			Juvenile steelhead				
23	Differ by group and site	394.16	9.70	30	-167.08	na	na
24	Differ by group, equal by site	1906.76	1523.30	20	-933.38	1532.60 (8)	<0.0001
25	Equal by group, differ by site	384.44	0.00	22	-170.22	6.28 (8)	0.6159
26	Equal by group and site	1917.35	1532.90	18	-940.67	1547.18 (12)	<0.0001
			Subyearling Chinook salmon				
27	Differ by group and site	397.50	0.93	31	-167.75	na	na
28	Differ by group, equal by site	917.02	520.45	21	-437.51	539.52 (10)	<0.0001
29	Equal by group, differ by site	396.57	0.00	23	-175.29	15.08 (8)	0.0576
30	Equal by group and site	935.80	539.23	19	-448.90	562.30 (12)	<0.0001

Table 7. Detection probability estimates from an acoustic telemetry evaluation of dam-passage survival at The Dalles Dam, Oregon, 2010, based on the full model of detection probabilities.

[Estimated standard errors are in parentheses. Estimates are from models 19, 23, and 27 in table 7]

Release group	Detection site				
	rkm 275	rkm 234	rkm 153	rkm 86	rkm 49 to rkm 3
			Yearling Chinook salmon		
V_1	0.9995 (0.0005)	0.9950 (0.0017)	0.8080 (0.0095)	0.9393 (0.0058)	0.9480 (0.0054)
R_2		0.9944 (0.0028)	0.8025 (0.0148)	0.9370 (0.0091)	0.9530 (0.0080)
R_3		0.9973 (0.0019)	0.7973 (0.0147)	0.9285 (0.0095)	0.9388 (0.0089)
			Juvenile steelhead		
V_1	0.9984 (0.0009)	0.9972 (0.0013)	0.7457 (0.0106)	0.9272 (0.0064)	0.9418 (0.0061)
R_2		0.9986 (0.0014)	0.7779 (0.0153)	0.9299 (0.0095)	0.9489 (0.0085)
R_3		0.9959 (0.0024)	0.7620 (0.0158)	0.9201 (0.0101)	0.9325 (0.0098)
			Subyearling Chinook salmon		
V_1	0.9995 (0.0005)	0.9463 (0.0050)	0.8551 (0.0079)	0.9562 (0.0046)	0.9349 (0.0057)
R_2		0.9271 (0.0095)	0.8597 (0.0128)	0.9497 (0.0082)	0.9507 (0.0080)
R_3		0.9130 (0.0102)	0.8728 (0.0122)	0.9541 (0.0077)	0.9352 (0.0092)

Table 8. Detection probability estimates from an acoustic telemetry evaluation of dam-passage survival at The Dalles Dam, Oregon, 2010, based on reduced models of detection probabilities.

[Estimated standard errors are in parentheses. Estimates are from models 21, 25, and 29 in table 7]

Release group	Detection array				
	rkm 275	rkm 234	rkm 153	rkm 86	rkm 49 to rkm 3
			Yearling Chinook salmon		
V_1	0.9999 (0.0005)	0.9950 (0.0012)	0.8043 (0.0070)	0.9362 (0.0043)	0.9470 (0.0043)
R_2		0.9950 (0.0012)	0.8043 (0.0070)	0.9362 (0.0043)	0.9470 (0.0043)
R_3		0.9950 (0.0012)	0.8043 (0.0070)	0.9362 (0.0043)	0.9470 (0.0043)
			Juvenile steelhead		
V_1	0.9984 (0.0009)	0.9972 (0.0009)	0.7570 (0.0076)	0.9262 (0.0047)	0.9413 (0.0044)
R_2		0.9972 (0.0009)	0.7570 (0.0076)	0.9262 (0.0047)	0.9413 (0.0044)
R_3		0.9972 (0.0009)	0.7570 (0.0076)	0.9262 (0.0047)	0.9413 (0.0044)
			Subyearling Chinook salmon		
V_1	0.9995 (0.0005)	0.9350 (0.0041)	0.8599 (0.0059)	0.9534 (0.0036)	0.9383 (0.0042)
R_2		0.9350 (0.0041)	0.8599 (0.0059)	0.9534 (0.0036)	0.9383 (0.0042)
R_3		0.9350 (0.0041)	0.8599 (0.0059)	0.9534 (0.0036)	0.9383 (0.0042)

Table 9. Reach-specific survival estimates from the virtual/paired-release model from an acoustic telemetry evaluation of dam passage survival at The Dalles Dam, Oregon, 2010, based on the full model of detection and survival probabilities.

[Estimated standard errors are in parentheses. The dam-passage survival estimates prior to adjustment for tag life (S_{Dam} unadjusted) for The Dalles Dam also are shown. Reach survival estimates without adjustments for tag life (S_1–S_5) were from models 5, 7, and 13 in table 5]

Survival parameter	Release group		
	V_1	R_2	R_3
Yearling Chinook salmon			
S_1	0.9396 (0.0053)		
S_2	0.9825 (0.0030)	0.9614 (0.0069)	0.9863 (0.0041)
S_3	0.9529 (0.0051)	0.9412 (0.0086)	0.9537 (0.0076)
S_4	0.9926 (0.0024)	0.9987 (0.0017)	0.9954 (0.0029)
S_5	0.9938 (0.0021)	0.9934 (0.0033)	0.9961 (0.0029)
S_{Dam} unadjusted		0.9640 (0.0096)	
Juvenile steelhead			
S_1	0.9517 (0.0047)		
S_2	0.9755 (0.0035)	0.9688 (0.0062)	0.9701 (0.0060)
S_3	0.9377 (0.0059)	0.9582 (0.0074)	0.9493 (0.0080)
S_4	0.9850 (0.0036)	0.9902 (0.0042)	0.9952 (0.0031)
S_5	0.9869 (0.0036)	0.9958 (0.0037)	0.9999 (0.0036)
S_{Dam} unadjusted		0.9529 (0.0097)	
Subyearling Chinook salmon			
S_1	0.9210 (0.0055)		
S_2	0.9794 (0.0033)	0.9707 (0.0063)	0.9912 (0.0040)
S_3	0.9332 (0.0057)	0.9556 (0.0078)	0.9591 (0.0076)
S_4	0.9814 (0.0033)	0.9904 (0.0041)	0.9839 (0.0050)
S_5	0.9875 (0.0028)	0.9746 (0.0062)	0.9930 (0.0038)
S_{Dam}		0.9404 (0.0091)	

Model Averaging to Assess Equal Survival of Release Groups in Common Reaches

Model-selection uncertainty in the assessment of the assumption of equal survivals among release groups in common reaches suggested a model-averaging approach was appropriate. For example, results in table 5 indicate nearly equal support for the hypotheses of different and equal survivals of juvenile steelhead in common reaches and considerable support for several other hypotheses. The results of model selection were similar in data from subyearling Chinook salmon. We acknowledged the model-selection uncertainty by averaging the predicted survivals and standard errors from each of the species-specific models of survival in table 5 after weighting by the model weights of each model (table 11). We also used the most parsimonious models of detection probability (models 21, 25, and 29 in table 6) in this process.

Table 10. Reach-specific survival estimates from the virtual/paired-release model from an acoustic telemetry evaluation of dam passage survival at The Dalles Dam, Oregon, 2010, based on a reduced model of detection probabilities.

[Estimated standard errors are in parentheses. The dam-passage survival estimates prior to adjustment for tag life (S_{Dam} unadjusted) for The Dalles Dam also are shown. Reach survival estimates without adjustments for tag-life (S_1–S_5) were obtained from models 21, 25, and 29 in table 7]

	Release group		
Survival parameter	V_1	R_2	R_3
	Yearling Chinook salmon		
S_1	0.9396 (0.0053)		
S_2	0.9824 (0.0030)	0.9613 (0.0069)	0.9864 (0.0041)
S_3	0.9530 (0.0051)	0.9412 (0.0086)	0.9536 (0.0076)
S_4	0.9926 (0.0024)	0.9987 (0.0017)	0.9954 (0.0029)
S_5	0.9938 (0.0022)	0.9935 (0.0033)	0.9959 (0.0029)
S_{Dam} unadjusted		0.9642 (0.0096)	
	Juvenile steelhead		
S_1	0.9517 (0.0047)		
S_2	0.9755 (0.0035)	0.9688 (0.0062)	0.9701 (0.0060)
S_3	0.9375 (0.0059)	0.9584 (0.0075)	0.9494 (0.0080)
S_4	0.9853 (0.0035)	0.9900 (0.0043)	0.9952 (0.0031)
S_5	0.9870 (0.0035)	0.9964 (0.0037)	0.9989 (0.0034)
S_{Dam} unadjusted		0.9529 (0.0097)	
	Subyearling Chinook salmon		
S_1	0.9210 (0.0055)		
S_2	0.9802 (0.0033)	0.9704 (0.0063)	0.9902 (0.0040)
S_3	0.9323 (0.0058)	0.9560 (0.0078)	0.9604 (0.0074)
S_4	0.9815 (0.0033)	0.9903 (0.0041)	0.9836 (0.0050)
S_5	0.9873 (0.0028)	0.9752 (0.0062)	0.9928 (0.0037)
S_{Dam} unadjusted		0.9398 (0.0091)	

The reach-specific estimates of survival supported the model selection results. There were small differences among the model-averaged group-specific survival estimates of yearling Chinook salmon in the S_3, S_4, and S_5 reaches (range 0.0004 to 0.0430 based on data in table 12), as expected based on the support for the model of equal groups survivals within reaches (model 32 in table 11). Model-averaged estimates of reach-specific survival were also similar among release groups for juvenile steelhead and subyearling Chinook salmon. The V_1 group survivals were slightly lower than those of the other groups in some reaches, but the largest difference was 0.0258 (subyearling Chinook salmon in the S_3 reach).

Table 11. Models used to evaluate hypotheses about the equality of reach-specific survivals of release groups in reaches they had in common from an acoustic telemetry evaluation of dam-passage survival at The Dalles Dam, Oregon, 2010, based on reduced models of detection probability.

[Data include Akaike's information criterion (AIC), the differences in AIC relative to the AIC best model in the set (Delta AIC), the number of parameters estimated by each model (K), the model likelihood, and the model weight. Detection probabilities are per models 21, 25, and 29 in table 7]

Model No.	Hypothesis	AIC	Delta AIC	K	Model Likelihood	Model Weight
		Yearling Chinook salmon				
31	Groups differ within all reaches	314.64	6.89	23	0.032	0.031
32	Groups equal within S_3, S_4, S_5	307.75	0.00	17	1.000	0.969
		Juvenile steelhead				
33	Groups differ within all reaches	384.44	0.32	22	0.852	0.262
34	Groups equal within S_3, S_4, S_5	388.76	4.64	16	0.098	0.030
35	Groups equal in S_5	386.75	2.63	20	0.268	0.083
36	Groups equal in S_4	384.12	0.00	20	1.000	0.308
37	Groups equal within S_3, S_4	385.72	1.60	18	0.449	0.138
38	Groups equal in S_3	385.21	1.09	20	0.580	0.179
		Subyearling Chinook salmon				
39	Groups differ within all reaches	396.57	1.69	23	0.430	0.255
40	Groups equal within S_3, S_4, S_5	404.58	9.70	17	0.008	0.005
41	Groups equal in S_5	399.3	4.42	21	0.110	0.065
42	Groups equal in S_4	394.88	0.00	21	1.000	0.593
43	Groups equal within S_3, S_4	402.11	7.23	19	0.027	0.016
44	Groups equal in S_3	399.25	4.37	21	0.112	0.067

Table 12. Model-averaged reach-specific survival estimates from the virtual/paired-release model from an acoustic telemetry evaluation of dam passage survival at The Dalles Dam, Oregon, 2010.

[Estimated standard errors are in parentheses. Reach survival estimates without adjustments for tag life (S_3–S_5) were based on model-averaged results from table 10]

Survival parameter	Release group		
	V_1	R_2	R_3
	Yearling Chinook salmon		
S_3	0.9815 (0.0060)	0.9502 (0.0043)	0.9506 (0.0040)
S_4	0.9518 (0.0082)	0.9948 (0.0017)	0.9947 (0.0016)
S_5	0.9946 (0.0015)	0.9942 (0.0016)	0.9943 (0.0016)
	Juvenile steelhead		
S_3	0.9399 (0.0074)	0.9539 (0.0091)	0.9484 (0.0073)
S_4	0.9868 (0.0037)	0.9895 (0.0035)	0.9922 (0.0042)
S_5	0.9874 (0.0043)	0.9960 (0.0038)	0.9983 (0.0039)
	Subyearling Chinook salmon		
S_3	0.9328 (0.0061)	0.9551 (0.0089)	0.9586 (0.0092)
S_4	0.9829 (0.0030)	0.9863 (0.0045)	0.9837 (0.0036)
S_5	0.9872 (0.0028)	0.9762 (0.0065)	0.9923 (0.0040)

Tag Life Adjustments and Dam-Survival Estimates

Adjustments for differences in fish travel time probabilities and tag life probabilities resulted in slight increases in reach-specific survival estimates of yearling Chinook salmon and juvenile steelhead, but those of subyearling Chinook salmon were unchanged. Tag-life-adjusted reach-specific survival estimates were less than or equal to 0.0089 higher than unadjusted estimates (table 13). The uncorrected reach-specific survivals were identical to those from the University of Washington (J. Skalski, University of Washington, written commun., November 19, 2010). The tag-life probabilities used in the adjustment for each release group differed slightly from those of the University of Washington, but were within 0.0008 of one another (J. Skalski, University of Washington, written commun., November 19, 2010). The tag-life-adjusted dam-survival estimate was 0.9641 (SE 0.0096) for yearling Chinook salmon and 0.9534 (SE 0.0097) for juvenile steelhead. These point estimates are within 0.0001 of the estimates from the University of Washington and have the same standard errors as those from University of Washington (J. Skalski, University of Washington, written commun., November 19, 2010). The tag-life adjusted reach and dam-survival estimates for subyearling Chinook salmon were identical to the unadjusted estimates, because the tag lives exceeded all but one of the travel times. The shortest tag life of those tested was 31.3 d, the longest fish travel time recorded was 34.2 d, and the second longest was 28.7 d. The tag-life-adjusted dam-survival estimate of subyearling Chinook salmon was 0.9404 (SE 0.0091).

Table 13. Unadjusted and tag-life adjusted reach-specific survival and dam-survival estimates from an acoustic telemetry evaluation of dam-passage survival at The Dalles Dam, Oregon, 2010.

[SE denotes standard error. na denotes not applicable]

Release group	Reach	Unadjusted Reach survival	Unadjusted Dam survival	Tag Life adjustment ($\hat{T}$)	Adjusted Reach survival Estimate	Adjusted Reach survival SE	Adjusted Dam survival Estimate	Adjusted Dam survival SE
				Yearling Chinook salmon				
V_1	Rkm 309 to rkm 275	0.9396	0.9640	0.9990	0.9405	0.0053	0.9641	0.0096
R_2	Rkm 307 to rkm 234	0.9614	na	0.9908	0.9703	0.0059	na	na
R_3	Rkm 275 to rkm 234	0.9863	na	0.9917	0.9946	0.0042	na	na
				Juvenile steelhead				
V_1	Rkm 309 to rkm 275	0.9517	0.9530	0.9990	0.9527	0.0048	0.9534	0.0097
R_2	Rkm 307 to rkm 234	0.9688	na	0.9908	0.9778	0.0077	na	na
R_3	Rkm 275 to rkm 234	0.9701	na	0.9914	0.9786	0.0074	na	na
				Subyearling Chinook salmon				
V_1	Rkm 309 to rkm 275	0.9210	0.9404	1.0000	0.9210	0.0055	0.9404	0.0091
R_2	Rkm 307 to rkm 234	0.9707	na	1.0000	0.9707	0.0064	na	na
R_3	Rkm 275 to rkm 234	0.9912	na	1.0000	0.9912	0.0040	na	na

Discussion

The analyses we conducted independent from the ATLAS software resulted in estimates of tag-life-adjusted dam survival that were nearly identical to those from the University of Washington using the ATLAS software. The estimates for juvenile steelhead and subyearling Chinook salmon were equal between analytical methods and the estimates for yearling Chinook salmon were within 0.0001 of one another, with our estimate 0.9641 (SE 0.0096) being greater than that from the University of Washington. The standard errors of the estimates from each group were identical. The reason for the 0.0001 difference in estimates for yearling Chinook salmon is likely the difference in the methods used for the adjustment for tag-life probabilities. We used a different method to estimate the variance components and used the R software (R Development Core Team, 2009) to model the tag-life probabilities, whereas the University of Washington used the ATLAS software written in C++. The ATLAS software retains a larger number of significant digits than the R software, which likely contributed to the differences in tag-life adjustments and resulting difference in adjusted dam-survival estimates from yearling Chinook salmon.

There did not appear to be an effect of tagger skill on estimates of survival, but the analysis was confounded by allocation of tagger effort. A very uniform allocation of tagger effort was evident in data from the spring study period, but not in the summer study period. Uneven allocation of effort resulted in what at first appeared to be an indication that some taggers were more skilled than others, based on the survival of fish they tagged. However, because the effort of some taggers was concentrated early in the study and that of others was concentrated late, any potential tagger effect was confounded with a potential seasonal trend in survival. Analysts at the University of Washington were unable to separate these effects due to the confounding of uneven allocation of tagger effort through time and other seasonal effects (John Skalski, University of Washington, written commun., November 5, 2010). Equal allocation of tagger effort across time and among release groups is important in studies of survival to enable the testing of tagger effects as well as to spread the risk of differences among tagger skill evenly across the study groups.

The observed data supported models that included differences in reach-specific survival of juvenile steelhead and subyearling Chinook salmon V_1, R_2, and R_3 release groups in each of the reaches downstream of Bonneville Dam (S_3, S_4, S_5), violating one model assumption. There was considerable model-selection uncertainty with respect to where the differences occurred, so we based our interpretation of the data on model-averaged results. These results indicate small differences between the survival of V_1 groups relative to the other release groups, but the differences in estimated reach-specific survival were small and ranged from 0.0034 to 0.0258. Thus, although the survival estimates of the V_1 groups of juvenile steelhead and subyearling Chinook salmon were usually lower than the other release groups in the reaches downstream of Bonneville Dam, the differences are likely not biologically meaningful. Moreover, differences among the release groups in survival downstream of Bonneville Dam do not affect the estimates of dam survival, because dam survival is estimated using data only from reaches upstream of Bonneville Dam.

The use of a reduced, more parsimonious, model of detection probabilities rather than the full model had little effect on the dam-survival estimates and did not improve their precision. The dam-survival estimates based on the full and reduced models of detection probabilities were equal for juvenile steelhead, differed by 0.0001 for yearling Chinook salmon and 0.0006 for subyearling Chinook salmon. The standard errors were identical between methods. As a general rule, reducing the number of parameters to be estimated from a given dataset is expected to result in improved precision for the parameters that are estimated. The lack of a benefit in this particular study is likely due to the large sample sizes, high recapture probabilities and high survival probabilities. The general rule suggests that the quality of information is improved when extra parameters are not estimated unnecessarily (for example, only a single common detection parameter is estimated for two groups when the data indicate that the true probability does not differ between groups). However, if there is not much loss of precision, as in this study, there may be a benefit in using a full model in that no model selection is required. Besides potentially increased precision, a reduced model also might have a slightly different point estimate of a critical parameter. Estimates of survival are now commonly compared to a stipulated standard. If interested parties can agree on the models that will be evaluated before data are even collected (that is, that specific multiple models or only a fully parameterized model will be used to estimate parameters) the potential for conflicting results from competing models can be avoided (Anderson and others, 1999).

The virtual/paired-release survival model was designed as an improvement to the paired-release models used in many previous studies, but it may not perform as expected under all circumstances. Paired-release models described by Burnham and others (1987), including the route-specific survival model of Skalski and others (2002), have been commonly used in the Columbia River Basin and rely on two release groups homologous to the V_1 and R_2 groups of the new model. The goal of the new model is to adjust the estimate of dam survival for short-term handling mortality experienced by the R_2 release group but not by the V_1 release group. In previous models, such handling mortality was hypothesized to positively bias estimates of dam survival. Thus, the new model should adjust the estimate of dam survival downward relative to a paired-release approach, but this was not always the case in the data we examined. The dam-survival estimate of juvenile steelhead from the virtual/paired-release model was lower than the estimate calculated from the paired-release model, which is the expected result based on the hypothesis of differential handling mortality expressed by R_2 and V_1 (results prior to tag life correction = 0.9530 virtual/paired release versus 0.9675 paired release; paired-release analyses not shown). For yearling or subyearling Chinook salmon, however, we found that the virtual/triple released model produced estimates that were higher than the paired-release model, which is contrary to the expected result (yearling Chinook salmon results prior to tag life correction = 0.9640 virtual/paired release versus 0.9589 paired release; subyearling Chinook salmon results prior to tag life correction = 0.9404 virtual/paired release versus 0.9327 paired release).

One case that can result in an elevated S_{Dam} estimate from the virtual/paired-release model relative to the paired-release model is when there is little or no tagging and handling mortality in R_2 or R_3 release groups. The virtual/paired release model assumes (1) tagging and handling mortality is fully expressed in the R_2 and R_3 groups prior to detection at Bonneville Dam and (2) that it is equal in both groups. In this study, the R_2 group traveled 73 km from release in the tailrace of The Dalles Dam prior to detection at Bonneville Dam and the R_3 group traveled 41 km from release near Hood River, Oregon, prior to detection at Bonneville Dam. Some tagging and handling mortality in the R_2 group should logically be expressed prior to the release point of the R_3 group, so in the presence of tagging and handling mortality $S_3 \leq S_{2.2}$ should always be the case if this source of mortality is equal between the two groups as assumed (see fig. 5 for diagram). If handling mortality is absent from R_2 and R_3 then $S_3 = S_{2.2}$ and random variation can result in $\hat{S}_3 > \hat{S}_{2.2}$ (notice the ^ indicating that these are the estimates of the true parameters). When $\hat{S}_3 > \hat{S}_{2.2}$ the virtual/paired-release model will inflate the estimate of dam survival from that of the paired release model, which is contrary to the goal of adjusting a paired-release estimate downward to account for handling mortality. To make this point, we show how S_{Dam} from the

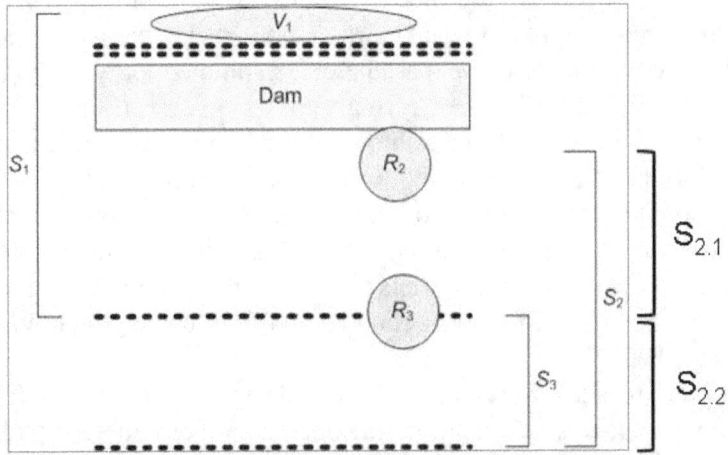

Figure 5. Modified schematic of the virtual/paired release model from Skalski (2009). The survival of the R_2 group (S_2) has been divided into two sections ($S_{2.1}$, $S_{2.2}$) to enable discussion of model assumptions and the proposed model adjustment to prevent dam survival estimates greater than those from paired-release models. Dashed lines represent detection sites.

$$\hat{S}_{dam} = \frac{\hat{S}_1}{\left(\dfrac{\hat{S}_2}{\hat{S}_3}\right)} = \hat{S}_1\left(\frac{\hat{S}_3}{\hat{S}_2}\right) = \hat{S}_1\left(\frac{\hat{S}_3}{\hat{S}_{21}\hat{S}_{22}}\right) = \left(\frac{\hat{S}_1}{\hat{S}_{21}}\right)\left(\frac{\hat{S}_3}{\hat{S}_{22}}\right)$$

$\underbrace{\hspace{5cm}}$

Virtual/paired-release model

Paired-release model   Adjustment

Figure 6. Equation showing that the virtual/paired release model of Skalski (2009) is an adjustment of the paired release model. The intent of the virtual/paired release model is to adjust the paired release model downward to account for tagging and handling mortality when $S_3/S_{22} < 1$. See figs. 1 and 5 for parameter definitions.

virtual/paired release model can be expressed as a correction to S_{Dam} estimated from a paired release model (fig. 6). If $S_3/S_{22} \leq 1$, then this provides evidence of handling mortality and the virtual/paired-release model will appropriately adjust the estimate of S_{Dam} downward from that of the paired-release model. However, $S_3/S_{22} > 1$ suggests no evidence of a handling effect and the correction to the paired-release model will result in a greater estimate of survival than the paired-release model, which is contrary to the intent. This process addresses the case when there is little or no tagging and handling mortality present, but it does not address whether or not that source of mortality is equal between the R_2 and R_3 groups.

Another case that can result in unexpected results is when tagging and handling mortality in R_2 and R_3 groups is unequal. In this case, the adjustment to the paired-release model will be affected. Possible mechanisms for unequal tagging and handling mortality include incomplete expression of tagging and handling mortality in the R_3 group between Hood River and Bonneville Dam, or if there were non-compensatory effects of tagging and handling that were different for the two release groups. The data and models examined support equality of survivals of the groups of yearling Chinook salmon downstream of Bonneville Dam (table 10) suggesting that tagging and handling mortality was fully expressed at Bonneville Dam, but there was considerable model selection uncertainty in data from subyearling Chinook salmon. The model-averaged reach-specific survival estimates show that the R_2 and R_3 group survivals of the Chinook salmon groups were nearly identical downstream of Bonneville Dam, also supporting full expression of tagging and handling mortality by the time fish passed Bonneville Dam (table 11). Non-compensatory effects could arise from differential selective pressures in the release areas. This could occur if selective pressures, such as predation, were different for the R_2 and R3 groups. One may expect this to most likely occur shortly after release, assuming acute expression of tagging or handling effects makes fish more susceptible to predation during that time. In the design of the study in 2010, the R_2 group was released near the tailrace of The Dalles Dam and the R3 group was released near Hood River, Oregon. Predation of juvenile salmonids is known to be greater near dam forebays and tailraces compared to mid-reservoir areas, which is consistent with this hypothesis (Petersen, 1994; Ward and others, 1995). Greater tagging and handling mortality in the R_2

group than the R3 group based on spatial patterns of predation (greater in the tailrace of The Dalles Dam than in mid-reservoir) would result in a positive bias in the estimate of S_{Dam} from the virtual/paired release model. This would arise because the R3 group would account for less than the total tagging and handling mortality of the R_2 group, resulting in a situation analogous to the potential drawback of the paired-release model. We pose this as a hypothesis, because there is no empirical data with which to determine if it occurred.

These issues are important to consider, because even small differences in estimates of dam survival can affect compliance with BIOP survival standards. The model adjustment in figure 6 resulted in an unintended upward adjustment of the S_{Dam} estimates for yearling and subyearling Chinook salmon at The Dalles Dam in 2010, because for these groups $\hat{S}_3 > \hat{S}_{22}$ indicating the lack of detectable tagging and handling mortality (yearling Chinook salmon adjustment = 0.9863/0.9811 = 1.0053; subyearling Chinook salmon adjustment = 0.9912/0.9830 = 1.0083). In these cases, it may have been more appropriate to use the result of the paired release model. This would have resulted in $\hat{S}_{dam}$ prior to tag life correction of 0.9589 for yearling Chinook salmon and 0.9327 for subyearling Chinook salmon. Inasmuch as there was very little effect of the tag life correction for these data, this would have changed the outcome for yearling Chinook salmon from passing to failing the performance standard of $S_{Dam} \geq$ 0.96, but left the outcome of subyearling Chinook salmon meeting the performance standard of $S_{Dam} \geq$ 0.93 unchanged.

In summary, our analyses resulted in nearly identical dam-survival estimates at The Dalles Dam as those from the University of Washington group, despite using different analytical tools. The 0.0001 difference in the tag-life adjusted dam-survival estimates of juvenile steelhead between the two groups may be due to slight differences in the tag-life adjustment methods and the precision of the software used to estimate them. The model assumption stipulating all release groups should have equal survivals in reaches they have in common (A8) was violated in data from juvenile steelhead and subyearling Chinook salmon, but occurred due to small differences in the reach-specific estimates and in reaches downstream of those used in estimating dam survival. We hypothesize that low tagging and handling mortality relative to the precision of the estimates of S_2 and S_3 for Chinook salmon caused an increase in estimated dam survival over that expected from the paired release model, and pose the hypothesis that differential selective pressures near release sites of R_2 and R_3 groups could bias estimates of S_{Dam} from the virtual/paired release model, which should be investigated further.

Acknowledgments

This study was made possible by the collaboration of many people. Staff at the Pacific Northwest National Laboratory carried out the field work for the study at The Dalles Dam and provided proofed data for our analyses. Dr. John Skalski and his staff at the University of Washington developed the virtual/paired-release model and worked with Pacific Northwest National Laboratory to plan the field work. He and his staff also wrote the ATLAS software package, which they used for their analysis of the data. Our analyses were completed with open communication with Dr. Skalski and his staff, which ensured that both groups had the same data and information for their analyses. The report was improved with comments from Dr. David Hewitt and an anonymous reviewer. We thank our colleagues at the Western Fisheries Research Center for contributing to this research product. Funding for this project was provided by the U.S. Army Corps of Engineers, Portland District, Portland, Oregon, contracts WK66QKZ01246253 and W66QKZ01246254.

References Cited

Anderson, D.A., Burnham, K.P., Franklin, A.B., Gutiérrez, R.B., Forsman, E.D., Anthony, R.G., White, G.C., and Shenk, T.M., 1999, A protocol for conflict resolution in analyzing empirical data related to natural resource controversies: Wildlife Society Bulletin, v. 27, no., 4, p. 1050–1058.

Burnham, K.P., and Anderson, D.R., 2002, Model selection and multimodel inference: A practical information-theoretic approach: New York, Springer-Verlag, 488 p.

Burnham, K.P., Anderson, D.R., White, G.C., Brownie, C., and Pollock, K.H., 1987, Design and analysis methods for fish survival experiments based on release-recapture: American Fisheries Society, America Fisheries Society Monograph, v. 5, 737 p.

Carlson, T.J., 2009, Acoustic telemetry evaluation of dam-passage survival and associated metrics at John Day, The Dalles, and Bonneville Dams, 2010: Draft report to the U.S. Army Corps of Engineers, Portland, Oregon.

Carlson, T.J., and Skalski, J.R., 2010, Compliance monitoring of juvenile yearling Chinook salmon and steelhead survival and passage at The Dalles Dam, spring 2010: Pacific Northwest National Laboratory and University of Washington, PNNL-19819.

Cormack, R.M., 1964, Estimates of survival from the sighting of marked animals: Biometrika, v. 51, no. 3–4, p. 429–438.

Jolly, G.M., 1965, Explicit estimates from capture-recapture data with both death and immigration-stochastic model: Biometrika, v. 52, no. 1–2, p. 225–247.

Lady, J.M., and Skalski, J.R., 2009, USER 4: User specified estimation routine: Prepared for the U.S. Department of Energy, Bonneville Power Administration, Project No. 198910700, Portland, Oregon. Available at *http://www.cbr.washington.edu/paramest/user/*.

Lady, J.W., Westhagen, P., and Skalski, J.R., 2010, Program ATLAS 1: Active tag-life adjusted survival: University of Washington, accessed April 3, 2011, at *http://www.cbr.washington.edu/paramest/atlas/*.

Li, T., and Anderson, J.J., 2009, The vitality model: A way to understand population survival and demographic heterogeneity: Theoretical Population Biology, v. 76, p. 118–131.

National Marine Fisheries Service, 2008, Endangered Species Act, Section 7(a)(2), Consultation Biological Opinion and Magnuson-Stevens Fishery Conservation and Management Act Essential Fish Habitat Consultation: NOAA, Log number F/NWR/2005/05883.

Petersen, J.H., 1994, Importance of spatial pattern in estimating predation of juvenile salmonids in the Columbia River: Transactions of the American Fisheries Society, v. 13, p. 924–930.

R Development Core Team, 2009, The R project for statistical computing: R Foundation for Statistical Computing, accessed April 3, 2011, at http://www.R-project.org.

Seber, G.A.F., 1965, A note on the multiple recapture census: Biometrika, v. 52, no. 1-2. p. 249–259.

Seber, G.A.F., 1982, The estimation of animal abundance and related parameters: New York, Macmillan, 654 p.

Skalski, J.R., 2009, Statistical design for the lower Columbia River acoustic-tag investigations of dam-passage survival and associated metrics: Report to the U.S. Army Corps of Engineers, Portland, Oregon.

Skalski, J.R., 2010, Appendix A: Statistical methods used in ATLAS: University of Washington, draft report.

Skalski, J.R., Townsend, R., Lady, J., Giorgi, A.E., Stevenson, J.R., and McDonald, R.S., 2002, Estimating route-specific passage and survival probabilities at a hydroelectric project from smolt radiotelemetry studies: Canadian Journal of Fisheries and Aquatic Sciences, v. 59, p. 1385–1393.

University of Washington, 2010, Active tag-life adjusted survival: University of Washington, accessed April 3, 2011, at *http://www.cbr.washington.edu/paramest/atlas/.* .

U.S. Army Corps of Engineers, Bonneville Power Administration, and U.S. Bureau of Reclamation, 2007, Biological assessment for effects of Federal Columbia River Power System and mainstem effects of other tributary actions on anadromous salmonid species listed under the Endangered Species Act: available at *http://www.salmonrecovery.gov,* 789 p.

Ward, D.L., Petersen, J.H., and Loch, J.J., 1995, Index of predation of juvenile salmonids by Northern Squawfish in the lower and middle Columbia River and in the lower Snake River: Transactions of the American Fisheries Society, v. 124, p. 321–334.

Appendix A. Detection History Categories and Counts from Yearling Chinook Salmon from an Acoustic Telemetry Evaluation of Dam-Passage Survival at The Dalles Dam, 2010

[A '9' in the category represents censoring]

Release group = V_1, total observed count = 2,037

Category	Counts	Category	Counts	Category	Counts
1000000	123	1100111	3	1101011	1
1100000	34	1190000	57	1101110	1
1101111	4	1110010	1	1110000	88
1110001	4	1110101	19	1110011	21
1110100	5	1111000	11	1110110	8
1110111	270	1111011	67	1111001	9
1111010	1	1111110	28	1111100	7
1111101	55	1011111	1	1111111	1219

Release group = R_2, total observed count = 796

Category	Counts	Category	Counts	Category	Counts
0200000	31	0210101	8	0210110	4
0201111	4	0211000	1	0211001	1
0210100	2	0211011	35	0211100	3
0210111	119	0211110	7	0211111	503
0211101	24	0210000	45		
0210010	1	0210011	8		

Release group = R_3, total observed count = 797

Category	Counts	Category	Counts	Category	Counts
0300000	11	0390000	1	0310000	37
0301111	2	0310010	1	0310011	12
0310100	3	0310101	11	0310110	3
0310111	121	0311000	3	0311001	2
0311010	1	0311011	37	0311100	1
0311101	31	0311110	17	0311111	503

Appendix B. Detection History Categories and Counts from Juvenile Steelhead from an Acoustic Telemetry Evaluation of Dam-Passage Survival at The Dalles Dam, 2010

[A '9' in the category represents censoring]

Release group = V_1, total observed count = 2,048					
Category	Counts	Category	Counts	Category	Counts
1000000	99	1111101	62	1101011	1
1100000	48	1190000	68	1101110	1
1100011	1	1110010	10	1110000	118
1101100	1	1110101	18	1110011	32
1101111	1	1111000	21	1110110	40
1110001	5	1111011	58	1111001	2
1110100	6	1111110	103	1111100	23
1110111	318	1010000	3	1111111	997
1111010	12				

Release group = R_2, total observed count = 799					
Category	Counts	Category	Counts	Category	Counts
0200000	25	0210101	8	0210110	8
0200110	1	0211000	6	0211001	2
0210001	1	0211011	31	0211100	6
0210111	132	0211110	49	0211111	456
0211010	4	0210000	34		
0211101	23	0210011	13		

Release group = R_3, total observed count = 798					
Category	Counts	Category	Counts	Category	Counts
0300000	24	0300001	1	0310000	40
0301111	2	0310010	1	0310011	16
0310001	3	0310101	8	0310110	20
0310100	1	0311000	3	0311001	2
0310111	124	0311011	30	0311100	4
0311010	5	0311110	48	0311111	436
0311101	30				

Appendix C. Capture History Categories and Counts from Subyearling Chinook Salmon from an Acoustic Telemetry Evaluation of Dam-Passage Survival at The Dalles Dam, 2010

[A '9' in the detection history denotes censoring]

Release group = V_1, total observed count = 2,417

Category	Count	Category	Count	Category	Count
1000000	191	1100111	10	1101110	3
1011101	1	1101101	4	1110000	141
1100000	54	1190000	31	1110011	11
1101100	3	1110101	30	1110110	6
1101111	86	1111000	32	1111001	5
1110100	2	1111011	66	1111100	22
1110111	226	1111110	41	1111111	1365
1111010	1	1101000	1		
1111101	83	1101011	2		

Release group = R_2, total observed count = 800

Category	Count	Category	Count	Category	Count
0200000	26	0200111	6	0201110	2
0201100	2	0210101	5	0210000	33
0201111	38	0211000	6	0210011	4
0210111	86	0211011	24	0210110	1
0211010	3	0211110	20	0211001	1
0211101	28	0201000	1	0211100	16
0200100	1	0201011	4	0211111	493

Release group = R_3, total observed count = 800

Category	Count	Category	Count	Category	Count
0300000	10	0301101	2	0301011	2
0300011	1	0390000	1	0301110	1
0301100	1	0310101	4	0310000	31
0301111	47	0311000	11	0310011	4
0310100	1	0311011	25	0310110	2
0310111	71	0311110	26	0311001	1
0311101	37	0300010	1	0311100	5
0300111	9	0300101	2	0311111	505

Appendix D. Daily Numbers of Yearling Chinook Salmon Tagged by Each Tagger during the Spring Study Period during an Acoustic Telemetry Evaluation of Dam-Passage Survival at The Dalles Dam, 2010

Date	Tagger Number					
	1	2	3	4	5	6
4/27/2010	0	25	0	24	23	0
4/28/2010	0	23	0	24	25	0
4/29/2010	0	32	0	32	33	0
4/30/2010	26	8	18	8	9	28
5/1/2010	25	25	18	24	26	29
5/2/2010	27	7	19	7	10	26
5/3/2010	53	0	40	0	0	54
5/4/2010	38	0	23	0	0	37
5/5/2010	53	0	37	0	0	56
5/6/2010	9	26	6	21	25	10
5/7/2010	26	24	19	23	24	29
5/8/2010	9	25	7	22	25	9
5/9/2010	0	47	0	49	51	0
5/11/2010	0	48	0	50	49	0
5/12/2010	27	41	18	42	40	27
5/13/2010	27	25	18	25	24	27
5/14/2010	26	9	20	7	9	26
5/15/2010	54	0	39	0	0	54
5/16/2010	36	0	26	0	0	35
5/17/2010	52	0	39	0	0	55
5/18/2010	9	24	6	23	24	10
5/19/2010	25	23	20	23	26	30
5/20/2010	9	24	7	23	25	9
5/21/2010	0	48	0	48	51	0
5/22/2010	0	33	0	32	32	0
5/23/2010	0	46	0	48	53	0
5/24/2010	25	8	19	8	9	28
5/25/2010	24	25	18	26	24	29
5/26/2010	25	9	18	7	9	29
5/27/2010	53	0	38	1	0	55
5/28/2010	31	0	20	0	0	32
5/29/2010	26	0	19	0	0	30
5/30/2010	10	0	7	0	0	8
5/31/2010	17	0	12	0	0	19

Appendix E. Daily Numbers of Juvenile Steelhead Tagged by Each Tagger during the Spring Study Period during an Acoustic Telemetry Evaluation of Dam-Passage Survival at The Dalles Dam, 2010

Date	Tagger Number					
	1	2	3	4	5	6
4/27/2010	0	24	0	23	24	0
4/28/2010	0	24	0	24	24	0
4/29/2010	0	32	0	30	35	0
4/30/2010	25	8	20	8	9	27
5/1/2010	26	24	19	25	26	27
5/2/2010	25	8	20	8	8	27
5/3/2010	55	0	40	0	0	54
5/4/2010	35	0	26	0	0	36
5/5/2010	54	0	41	0	0	52
5/6/2010	9	25	7	22	25	9
5/7/2010	28	24	20	24	24	27
5/8/2010	10	24	6	24	24	9
5/9/2010	0	49	0	49	49	0
5/11/2010	0	49	0	49	49	0
5/12/2010	26	39	18	41	41	27
5/13/2010	27	24	19	25	25	26
5/14/2010	27	7	18	10	8	27
5/15/2010	52	0	39	0	0	55
5/16/2010	34	0	26	0	0	37
5/17/2010	54	0	41	0	0	52
5/18/2010	9	24	7	24	24	9
5/19/2010	27	25	20	23	24	28
5/20/2010	9	23	6	25	24	10
5/21/2010	0	48	0	49	50	0
5/22/2010	0	33	0	33	31	0
5/23/2010	0	49	0	49	49	0
5/24/2010	25	8	20	8	9	27
5/25/2010	24	25	21	25	25	27
5/26/2010	24	8	20	8	9	28
5/27/2010	52	0	40	0	0	55
5/28/2010	29	0	23	0	0	31
5/29/2010	28	0	21	0	0	26
5/30/2010	9	0	7	0	0	9
5/31/2010	19	0	12	0	0	18

Appendix F. Daily Numbers of Subyearling Chinook Salmon Tagged by Each Tagger during the Summer Study Period during an Acoustic Telemetry Evaluation of Dam-Passage Survival at The Dalles Dam, 2010

[Tagger #5 did not tag subyearling Chinook salmon and taggers # 7 and #8 only tagged subyearling Chinook salmon]

Date	Tagger Number						
	1	2	3	4	6	7	8
6/12/2010	0	31	0	30	0	0	28
6/13/2010	0	30	0	30	0	0	28
6/14/2010	0	39	0	39	0	0	36
6/15/2010	0	38	0	38	0	0	38
6/16/2010	0	26	24	24	38	27	25
6/17/2010	0	7	45	8	0	44	9
6/18/2010	0	17	55	17	0	58	16
6/19/2010	0	0	32	0	47	35	0
6/20/2010	0	0	45	0	72	47	0
6/21/2010	0	30	6	30	11	7	29
6/22/2010	0	30	20	30	34	21	29
6/23/2010	0	30	7	30	12	7	29
6/24/2010	0	67	0	0	0	0	68
6/25/2010	0	38	0	40	0	0	36
6/26/2010	0	53	0	56	0	0	53
6/27/2010	0	9	34	8	56	0	8
6/28/2010	0	25	35	24	55	0	24
6/29/2010	30	9	23	8	36	0	8
6/30/2010	65	0	52	0	76	0	0
7/1/2010	39	0	30	0	43	0	0
7/2/2010	57	0	43	0	64	0	0
7/3/2010	41	28	7	28	10	0	0
7/4/2010	56	28	20	31	29	0	0
7/5/2010	42	26	7	29	9	0	0
7/6/2010	59	53	0	52	0	0	0
7/7/2010	0	56	0	58	0	0	0
7/8/2010	56	50	0	56	0	0	0
7/9/2010	47	8	24	8	0	0	27
7/10/2010	62	21	25	25	0	0	29
7/11/2010	45	8	25	8	0	0	28
7/12/2010	64	0	48	0	0	0	53
7/13/2010	46	0	34	0	0	0	35
7/14/2010	33	0	23	0	0	0	26
7/15/2010	10	0	8	0	0	0	11
7/16/2010	0	0	24	0	0	0	26

www.ingramcontent.com/pod-product-compliance
Lightning Source LLC
Chambersburg PA
CBHW080345290526
45791CB00009BA/2738